J14

ITI-BULLYING
BASICS

ANTI-BULLYING BASICS

BULLIED *by* Boys

WORLD
BOOK

A Scott Fetzer company
Chicago
worldbook.com

Staff

World Book, Inc.
233 North Michigan Avenue
Suite 2000
Chicago, Illinois, 60601 U.S.A.

For information about other World Book
publications, visit our website at
www.worldbook.com or call
1-800-967-5325.

The contents of this book were reviewed
by Kari A. Sassu, Ph.D., NCSP, assistant
professor, Counseling and School Psychology
Department, and coordinator, School
Psychology Program, Southern Connecticut
State University, New Haven, Connecticut.

Product development: Arcturus Publishing Ltd
Writer: Alex Woolf
Editor and picture researcher: Nicola Barber
Designer: Ian Winton

Executive Committee

President
Donald D. Keller
*Vice President and
Editor in Chief*
Paul A. Kobasa
*Vice President,
Sales and Marketing*
Sean Lockwood
Vice President, International
Richard Flower
Controller
Anthony Doyle
Director, Human Resources
Bev Ecker

Editorial

*Associate Director, Annuals
and Topical Reference*
Scott Thomas
*Managing Editor, Annuals and
Topical Reference*
Barbara A. Mayes
Senior Editor
Christine Sullivan
Administrative Assistant
Ethel Matthews
*Manager, Contracts & Compliance
(Rights & Permissions)*
Loranne K. Shields
Administrative Assistant
Gwen Johnson

Graphics and Design

Art Director
Tom Evans
Senior Designer
Don Di Sante
Media Researcher
Jeff Heimsath

Editorial Administration

Director, Systems and Projects
Tony Tills
*Senior Manager, Publishing
Operations*
Timothy Falk

Manufacturing/Production

Director
Carma Fazio
Manufacturing Manager
Steven K. Hueppchen
Production/Technology Manager
Anne Fritzinger
Proofreader
Nathalie Strassheim

Marketing

Manager
Tamika Robinson
Marketing Specialist
Annie Suhy

Library of Congress Cataloging-in-Publication Data

Bullied by boys.
    pages cm. -- (Anti-bullying basics)
    Includes index.
    Summary: "A discussion of bullying by boys, what causes bullying, how bullying affects bullies and their targets; contains advice
and useful strategies for targets of bullies"-- Provided by publisher.
    ISBN 978-0-7166-2071-6
    1. Bullying--Juvenile literature. 2. Aggressiveness--Juvenile literature. 3. Boys--Psychology--Juvenile literature.
4. Bullying--Prevention--Juvenile literature. I. World Book, Inc.
    BF637.B85B824 2014
    302.34'3--dc23
                                                  2013024681

World Book's Anti-Bullying Basics   Set ISBN: 978-0-7166-2070-9
Printed in China by PrintWORKS Global Services, Shenzhen, Guangdong
1st printing November 2013

Contents

What Is Bullying?

Bullying is unwanted, deliberately hurtful behavior that is repeated over a period of time. Bullying is often about an imbalance of power—bullies may use their physical strength, popularity, or something they know about another person to harm or control others.

Forms of bullying

Bullying can take many forms, including verbal, physical, social, and cyberbullying (a form of bullying on digital devices).

- Verbal bullying includes name-calling, teasing, inappropriate comments, threats, and abusive comments.
- Physical bullying includes hitting, kicking, spitting, tripping, and stealing or damaging possessions.
- Social bullying includes deliberately excluding someone from social events, spreading rumors about a person, and embarrassing or humiliating someone.
- Cyberbullying includes harassment and abuse via a cell phone, on social media sites, or online.

What bullying is not

Bullying is not:
- single occurrences of rejection, nastiness, or spite
- random acts of aggression
- one-time arguments or disagreements

All of these events can cause unhappiness. While falling out with friends or dealing with occasional disagreements may not be pleasant, they are a normal part of the process of learning and growing up. These occasional "dramas" in everyday life are very different from bullying, which is deliberate and repeated aggressive behavior that is intended to cause harm and unhappiness.

Why it's serious

Bullying is serious because it can have a damaging effect on the person being bullied, on the person doing the bullying, and even on the bystanders who witness incidents of bullying. Bullying creates a climate of fear, and bystanders may be anxious that they will be next on the bully's list of targets. The targets, the people who are being bullied, are more likely to lack self-confidence, have low self-esteem, have difficulty concentrating, and suffer from depression and anxiety. People who bully are at greater risk than others of becoming involved in violence and crime. Bullies also have a higher risk of struggling or failing at their school studies. Young people who are both bullies and bullied are at the highest risk of mental health problems later in life. And, both bullies and their targets may have a more difficult time forming healthy relationships as adults.

Why Do Boys Bully?

The vast majority of boys are not bullies. Most boys manage to negotiate the tricky path from childhood to manhood without feeling, or at least acting upon, the urge to repeatedly harm targeted people. A few boys, however, do get this urge, and if the opportunity arises, they become bullies.

Bullied by others

Boys sometimes become bullies because of difficult experiences. Some may be bullied themselves by their parents or by older siblings. Others may have witnessed bullying against members of their family. Exposure to such behavior can lead boys to believe that violence and aggression is normal and is the best way to get what they want.

Bullying behavior outside of school can result in boys becoming bullies to their peers at school.

Power play

Boys who are victims of physical abuse often feel powerless, angry, and insecure. Some boys become bullies to feel better about themselves. They may try to dominate other children in their class in order to feel strong and powerful—because when out of school they feel the opposite.

BULLYING Q & A

Why doesn't mom care?

Q. Things can get a little crazy in our house. I've got five brothers and there's always lots of shouting and fists flying. We're all scared of my eldest brother. He likes to be in control and he uses his fists a lot! Mom just laughs when we show her our bruises. She says "boys will be boys." She seems to think it's just the way boys are. Is she right?

A. No, she's not right. Boys are not naturally violent and most boys are not bullies. It's your mother's responsibility to protect you and she should be stopping your brother from bullying you, not encouraging it. If you can't get your mom to listen to your concerns, try talking to someone at your school, such as a guidance counselor. Your mom does care about you, but she may not realize how serious this problem can be for you and your brothers.

Tough guys

Boys can grow up feeling that being male is all about being tough and strong. Male action heroes, from Batman to James Bond, usually defeat their enemies with violence. Of course, men can also be caring and sympathetic, but these are not the main qualities associated with typical male role models. The "tough guy" image is very powerful in today's movie and gaming worlds, and some boys may take this image to mean that it's okay to bully.

The actor Daniel Craig as British agent James Bond. Bond represents an ideal of a male action hero. But the role has nothing to do with the actor.

What Sort of Boys Bully?

Male bullies can come from any background. They can be rich or poor and from any nationality. They can be aged 2 or 92, though most bullying occurs during adolescence (the years between childhood and adulthood). What bullies often have in common is a sense of frustration with their lives.

Insecure

Boy bullies are often insecure, and they attack others as a way of covering up their insecurity. They have a need to be in control, to make themselves appear powerful. They're also often attention-seekers. They think that by being mean to others, they will become more popular with the "cool" crowd.

Socially adept

Male bullies often have excellent social skills. They are good talkers and understand how to motivate and inspire, as well as scare, others. This helps them build up support and dominate those around them. What they lack, however, are relationship skills—things like patience, *empathy* (the ability to imagine and understand how others feel) and respect. Often, their only means of relating to their peers (people of their own age) is through mockery and intimidation.

"Good boys" can also be bullies

Boy bullies need a group of "followers" to give them strength and status. These followers do not start the bullying, but they often encourage it once it's begun, and they may even push the bully into greater acts of violence. Followers are not bullies when they are on their own and may generally be quite well behaved, but under the influence of a ringleader, these followers can become part of a "bullying pack."

Followers may encourage a ringleader once the bullying starts.

KING OF THE 7TH GRADE

Joe is a 7th-grader who lives in Chicago. His father is a doctor and his mother works in local politics. Joe is popular at school, but at home he feels neglected and unimportant. To feel better about himself, he's started bullying some of the kids in his class. His friends, and others who desperately want to be his friend, always support him when he picks on someone. He loves the feeling of power and respect that bullying gives him.

Physical Violence and Hazing

In general, boys and girls tend to bully in different ways. Boys often use physical violence, while girls are more likely to bully by making mean comments or by excluding the target of the bullying from their group.

Direct and indirect attacks

Boy bullies are often bigger and stronger than average, and they turn this to their advantage. They use physical violence to hurt, scare, intimidate, and humiliate their victims. Physical violence can include punching, kicking, shoving, pushing, shaking, tripping, poking, pinching, and slapping. It can also include indirect attacks, like throwing things at people, drenching them with water, or destroying, stealing, or spoiling their property.

Physical violence is the most visible form of bullying.

High-visibility bullying

Physical attacks are the most obvious kind of bullying and the easiest to spot. They usually occur in the open and are not pre-planned. Physical attacks create lots of noise, and they often leave evidence in the form of bruises or destroyed property. Because physical bullying is so visible and is often done by boys, it can seem that boys bully more than girls. However, girl bullies may be just as common—it's just that they engage in less visible forms of bullying.

Hazing

In some schools and colleges, kids establish *initiations* (joining ceremonies) for accepting a new member into their group. Sometimes, these ceremonies involve physical abuse and humiliation. This is called hazing, and it is very often a form of bullying. The worst examples of hazing include biting, cutting, burning, or whipping victims over a sustained period of time. In some extreme cases, hazing has resulted in serious injury and even death.

"MEET US AFTER TRAINING…"

Ben was 15 when his parents moved to New Jersey. Making friends at his new high school wasn't easy, but he enjoyed soccer and was excited to join the school team. Senior members of the team told him all rookies had to undergo an initiation ceremony and instructed him to meet them outside the locker room after practice. When he arrived, his teammates covered him with rotten food and turned high-pressure hoses on him. The next day, Ben reported them to the coach and the boys were punished. Ben decided not to join the school team after all, and he signed up with a local soccer club instead.

Verbal Bullying and Scare Tactics

Verbal bullying and *exclusion* (not allowing others to join in) is not just practised by girls. Boys can be very adept at using language as a weapon or hurting people by excluding them from their group. Boys are more likely than girls to use scare tactics—threatening violence or exclusion to scare someone into doing what they want.

Words that hurt

Physical violence is more easily spotted by teachers, so some boy bullies turn to verbal assaults to avoid getting into trouble. Verbal bullying includes name-calling, insults, and teasing. Sometimes this is done to the target's face, at other times behind his or her back. As with most forms of bullying, the aim is to humiliate the person while making the bully look dominant and powerful.

Tactics for dealing with verbal bullying include—

- ignoring the bully
- telling an adult
- remaining polite
- focusing on your friends

> Verbal bullying can be as hurtful as the physical kind.

Shunning

Children understand the power of exclusion from a very young age. "I'm not going to be your friend any more" is a common threat used by preschoolers. Exclusion bullying sends out a signal that this group is "cool," and you are not! It often leaves the targets feeling useless, lonely, and vulnerable.

Threats

"Don't tell or I'll punch you!" "Do it or I'll tell everyone you're a sissy!" Boy bullies are often good at manipulating people by the use of threats. For the bully, this is a very low-risk form of bullying, as it's usually just his word against the target's that anything was even said. Yet fear that the threat may actually be carried out can create a powerful hold over the person being bullied.

LUNCH MENACE

One morning, Josh stopped 10-year-old Sam in the school corridor. "Give me your lunch money or I'll beat you up," he demanded. Josh was a 6th grader and had a fierce reputation. Sam handed over the money and went home hungry. The next day, the same thing happened. The day after that, Sam asked his mom for extra money. Sam thought he could use the extra money to buy his own lunch and still hand over money to Josh. But Josh discovered the extra money and stole the lot. Weeks went by before Sam plucked up the courage to tell his mom what was happening. Sam's mom called the school principal and explained her son's problem. The principal met with Josh and began a plan where Josh went to see a school counselor twice a week to discuss his bullying problem. He never bullied Sam again.

Online Attacks

Boys often bully by sending mean messages through phone texts, e-mails, instant messaging, social networks, blogs, or chat rooms. This type of bullying is called cyberbullying.

Cyberbullies

Most boys use the Internet for friendly communication. For bullies, however, it provides a very easy way of intimidating, scaring, and humiliating a target. Unlike traditional bullying, cyberbullying can be done anonymously, without much risk to the bully. It can also be done 24 hours a day, seven days a week.

What do cyberbullies do?

Cyberbullies may send threatening e-mails, create hostile websites, post inaccurate and embarrassing items on blogs, or upload embarrassing photos of their targets. They may also socially exclude people by ignoring their messages or blocking them from online activities.

Cyberbullying can happen anywhere and at any time.

BULLYING Q & A

How do I stop this online humiliation?

Q. Soon after I stopped seeing my boyfriend, Mike, I started receiving unpleasant text messages from strangers. They called me terrible names. At school, kids were giving me odd looks. Eventually a friend told me that some photos of me had been uploaded to a public website. The pictures had been altered to make it look as if I was naked. They could only have come from Mike. I'm so angry and embarrassed. What can I do?

A. The first thing you should do is to tell an adult you trust—a family member, a school counselor, or teacher. In the United States, anyone connected with a school will have to report the incident if their state laws (or even school rules) require them to do so. That is not a bad thing, however, as people who work at schools should be trained to deal with a situation in which a child is being bullied.

Whoever helps you will likely be able to take action to remove the photos and punish Mike, if he's the one who did this. Don't reply to any unpleasant text messages, but don't delete them. It may be they will be needed as evidence. Finally, change your cell phone number to block the bullies who are sending you text messages.

Bullied by Family

Sometimes, the people bullying you are members of a group that should be supporting and helping you. People may be bullied by members of their family—their siblings (brothers and sisters).

All siblings fight

You may think it is natural for brothers and sisters to have conflicts. And, you are right. One study found that siblings fight among one another more than they fight with all other children combined. Siblings will often fight over a toy, a game, or over who gets to sit where. This fighting and competition between brothers and sisters is known as *sibling rivalry*. But if one sibling is always the one who starts the fights or calls the other names, and if one sibling is always the victim, it's possible the fighting is really bullying.

Fighting and competition between brothers is a natural part of growing up.

Who is more likely to be the bully in the family?

Nothing about people is true all the time. And that is as true of bullying as everything else. But, studies show that brothers tend to bully more often than sisters. One study found that being bullied by a sibling was more likely for both boys and girls who had an older brother. In addition, older children tend to bully siblings more often than younger children. The same study found that boys tended to bully in the home more often when they had a younger sibling. In addition to *gender* (male or female) and *birth order* (older or younger), the personality of a sibling matters. Children who lack empathy are more likely to bully.

TAKING SIBLING BULLYING SERIOUSLY

Parents will sometimes take the attitude that the fighting between their children is just a natural part of growing up. But if what they are ignoring is really bullying, there are good reasons to pay attention.

Children who bully siblings are far more likely to bully children who are peers at school. Childhood bullying is linked to higher levels of academic failure and to criminal behavior in later life. Children who are bullied by a sibling are more likely to be bullied by peers at school. Being bullied as a child is linked to emotional difficulties later in life.

A study published in 2013 stated that being bullied by a sibling is just as damaging psychologically as being bullied by a peer.

Racist and Homophobic Bullying

Young people from racial minority groups often experience bullying based on perceived differences in dress, language, appearance, beliefs, or *culture* (the traditions of a group of people with a shared identity or experience). Sometimes people are bullied because of their actual or imagined sexual orientation or gender identity. This is called *homophobic bullying*. It can take the form of cruel jokes, insults, exclusion, threats, humiliation, or physical violence.

Prejudice

Racial prejudice is usually caused by fear and ignorance about people of minority races. It may also be that people who hold racist attitudes have been exposed to, and influenced by, racist attitudes held by members of their family. Homophobic bullying is driven by fear of, dislike of, and ignorance about homosexuals. Being gay is a natural part of who a person is, just like a person's race. So homophobic bullying can be placed into the same category as racist bullying—they are both examples of prejudice.

Challenges faced by targets

Targets of racist bullying may feel afraid of speaking up because they feel a need to "fit in" and not draw attention to themselves. It's also possible that they don't trust the school authorities to take their complaint seriously, or they may be worried that talking about it will bring further trouble from the bullies for themselves and their family.

Gay people who experience homophobic bullying often keep quiet about it. This may be because they are ashamed, or they are worried about how friends or adults will react if they tell them why they are being bullied. It is particularly hard for people who have not "come out" about their gender preference or identity to their families, and who fear that their parents will react negatively to the news.

Targets of racist or homophobic bullying often find it hard to seek help.

CONFRONTING RACISM

David Chen, a 14-year-old Korean American boy, was picked on regularly by a group of boys at his school. They called him a "slant." They gave out his cell phone number, and he began to receive insulting text messages. David's friends started to desert him because they were scared of the bullies. His parents advised him to keep quiet and avoid trouble. Eventually, David found the courage to tell a teacher. The teacher took the matter very seriously. The bullies were punished and the whole school worked hard to combat racism. David was proud to take a leading role, speaking to other students about racism and becoming the school's anti-bullying coordinator.

Dealing with these forms of bullying

Schools can take steps to stamp out racist bullying and encourage targets to come forward without fear. This can be done through staff training, anti-racism workshops, and pairing students of different races together on projects. Workshops on tolerance and diversity can also help create a better atmosphere for gay students.

Bullies and Students with Disabilities

People who are disabled—especially people who are developmentally disabled—often have a more difficult time at school than their nondisabled peers. They hardly need people to bully them and make their time at school even more difficult. Nevertheless, one study showed that 60 percent of students with disabilities stated they had been bullied, compared to about 30 percent of nondisabled students.

Disabled kids most likely to be bullied

Children with developmental disabilities are more likely to be bullied than those with physical disabilities. Children with autism spectrum disorders (ASD) are often bullied by other children. ASD children can be socially awkward and can have difficulties communicating and relating to others. The more high-functioning an ASD child is, the more likely that child is to be bullied, as they are less likely to be in special-education classes and are more likely to be exposed to bullying when in mainstream classes.

If you are bullying a child in your class who to you seems "strange" or "different," it is possible you may be bullying someone whose brain is wired to work differently from yours. The child who has ASD has no more choice in the matter than you do about your eye color. And, that child is probably far less able to defend him- or herself than you are. Instead of teasing a child who is different, try being kind to that child. You may be surprised by how much better you feel about yourself.

Children with ASD may struggle at school.

BULLYING Q & A

How do I help my disabled child?

Q. My child has an autism spectrum disorder. He is being bullied by children in his class. They push him, make fun of the way he talks, and steal his things from him. It has gotten so he no longer wants to go to school. Is there any way I can help him?

A. If a disabled student is being bullied because of that disability, it can be considered harassment. Disabled students who have an Individualized Education Plan (IEP) qualify for the special protections given under U.S. federal law to the disabled. So do students who have a plan that gives students the right to the necessary accommodations to ensure their academic success. It is a serious matter if a school is aware that a disabled student is being bullied and takes no action. In such an instance, the U.S. Office for Civil Rights could find that a child is being denied an equal opportunity to education, which would be a serious issue for a school. Write a letter to your child's school telling them of the problem and your concerns, and request that the school intervene in this situation.

Bullying a child because of a disability is a serious issue.

Peer Pressure

Peer pressure is being influenced by people of your own age to go along with certain attitudes and behaviors. Sometimes this can be positive—your friends might encourage you to join a sports club or run for class officer. But peer pressure can be negative if it encourages children to participate in bullying.

Why is peer pressure so powerful?

Most of us have an urge to "fit in" and be liked by people of our age group. That's a perfectly natural and understandable feeling. However, bullies use this feeling to build up support. Others are encouraged to join in with the bullying to get the approval of the bully. If they don't join in, they fear that they too may end up being bullied.

Being part of a team can be a positive experience.

Pack mentality

Peer pressure can often lead to a "pack mentality." This is when kids encourage each other to commit much more serious acts of bullying than they would ever consider when alone. When a pack mentality develops, people often lose their judgment and common sense. If everyone's doing something, it's easier to feel less responsible for your actions. A pack mentality is particularly common in cyberbullying. Kids will pressure their friends to participate in online hate lists and mean blog posts.

BULLYING Q & A

How do I stand up to peer pressure?

Q. My friends have been teasing this girl about her weight. They laugh at her and call her names, then give me these looks when I don't join in. Now they've started ignoring me and not replying to my texts. I feel like I'm going to lose my friends if I don't play my part and pick on this girl—but I feel sorry for her.

....

A. It's tough to be the only one who says "no" to peer pressure, but you can do it. You know that what your friends are doing is wrong. Now you just need the self-confidence to stand firm and walk away. So what if you lose them as friends? Do you really want bullies as friends? Friends should be people you trust. Do you really trust this crowd? Talk to a trusted adult about what they're doing. Your responsibility is to yourself and the girl who is the target of bullying, not to these so-called friends.

Bystanders

Bullying usually involves more than the bully and the target. There are also the bystanders—those who watch the bullying happen. Bystanders provide the bully with the audience he craves. Their support, or even their silence, makes his behavior seem more acceptable.

How bystanders react

Bystanders can react in one of four ways. They can—

- stand and watch
- give support to the bully
- run away
- take action to try and stop the bullying.

The first three responses all give support to the bully. Bullies prefer a supportive audience—but if the audience just stands there, or if there's no audience at all, it won't necessarily stop them from bullying. The only thing that will discourage them is the fourth response: If the bystanders take action. Unfortunately, most bystanders don't do this. There are many possible reasons why.

· ·

Why don't bystanders intervene?

- they think it's none of their business
- they don't want to get hurt, too
- they feel frightened or powerless
- they don't like the target and think he or she deserves it
- the bully is a friend
- they don't want to draw attention to themselves
- they think that telling an adult will make the situation worse
- they don't want to be a tattletale
- they don't know what to do

All these reasons are understandable. Even so, not intervening while someone gets hurt puts the bystander on the same side as the bully. For some tips on what to do if you find yourself in this situation, see pages 38–39.

· ·

BULLYING Q & A

Why am I in trouble?

Q. I know Jeff can get a bit crazy sometimes, but he's a friend of mine. Even so, when he got Jon in a neckhold by the lockers the other day and started teasing him for being such a geek, I didn't join in. I didn't say or do anything bad to Jon. So why am I in trouble with the teachers now when I had nothing to do with it?

....

A. I'm afraid you did have something to do with it. By doing nothing, you gave support to Jeff. Imagine if Jon got seriously hurt and you "didn't do anything." Imagine if Jon got so desperate he tried to harm himself, and you "didn't do anything." Try to see things from Jon's point of view and then maybe you'll understand why not doing anything isn't good enough.

Talking to an adult about bullying behavior may help to put a stop to it.

The Effects of Bullying

Some people may think of bullying as a normal part of growing up, but bullying can have long-term, damaging effects. It can have an impact on a target's mental state and physical health, both at the time it occurs and later in life.

When the bullies aren't stopped...

Fear or embarrassment may prevent a target of bullying from talking to an adult. Even if he does speak up, some teachers or parents may excuse bullying as just "boys being boys." In these cases, when the bullies are allowed to continue with their behavior, they don't learn to change, and the bullying can go on for months, even years.

Short-term effects

Targets of bullying often suffer physical injuries and damage to property. Dread of the next incident may cause them stress, anxiety, and loss of sleep. The effects of stress can cause physical symptoms such as headaches or stomach problems. It can affect eating patterns, with some targets developing eating disorders or losing or gaining weight. At school, targets of bullying often find themselves friendless, and this can lead to feelings of isolation and low self-esteem. In extreme cases, the pain and suffering caused by bullying has led to suicide.

Long-term consequences

Targets of bullying often miss school either because of sickness or simply because they are afraid to go. All their energy goes into avoiding bullying, leaving little energy for their education. In the long term, this can result in lower grades, affecting college and career possibilities. Over the course of their lives, former targets of bullying may suffer from depression and emotional instability. Many find it difficult to form relationships.

BITTER MEMORIES

For years, Jerry suffered at the hands of a gang of bullying boys. In hallways and classrooms they tripped him and pushed him around. When he got home, it continued online. He'd get anonymous texts and e-mails, telling him he was "scum" and threatening him with beatings the following day. Jerry dropped out of high school before graduating. He suffered from anxiety and depression. Then, one day, a friend encouraged him to do something positive with his experiences instead of feeling bitter about them. Now he gives anti-bullying presentations to schools, describing what he went through and advising kids on how to deal with bullying.

Having someone to talk to
can help targets of bullying.

The Effects On Bullies

Bullying doesn't only leave its mark on the target; it affects the bully, too. Generally speaking, boys who bully do not simply outgrow their behavior. Their aggression often continues into adulthood. Studies have found a correlation, or a connection, between a person being a bully in childhood or adolescence and having a criminal record by their mid-20's. Bullying may not cause a person to become a criminal, but there is a link between them.

Bullying behavior may continue into adult life.

Craving power

One of the reasons boys become bullies in the first place is a need to exercise power over others. This need tends to continue into their grown-up years. But they may not find it as easy to dominate people in the workplace as they did in the playground, and this can lead to frustration and sometimes depression. Many former bullies struggle to get and keep jobs. They may abuse alcohol and drugs. Others get into trouble for fighting, stealing, and vandalism.

Antisocial behavior

Former bullies have a greater than average chance of suffering from an antisocial personality disorder. In other words, they may find it harder to *empathize with others* (imagine and understand their feelings). They are more likely to display delinquent behavior, violence, and aggression. Some children who bully may grow up to become abusive toward their spouses, partners, and children. Sadly, the children of bullies are more likely than other children to end up becoming bullies themselves.

A NEW START

Bill began bullying Tom in the 7th grade. Tom was lousy at sports, but good at art and science. Bill called him "fat" and "ugly" and abused him physically. Years later, Bill was stuck in a rut, unable to decide what to do with his life. At a high school reunion, he re-encountered Tom, now a successful architect. Bill apologized to him. He said he'd bullied him out of jealousy and because he was insecure. "I'm still insecure," he admitted, "and out of work." Tom said they had been awful years and he'd also struggled for a while after leaving school. In the end, what worked for him was self-belief. "Make a list of things you like about yourself and things you're good at," he suggested. Bill took Tom's advice to heart. Not long after, he enrolled in a training course to become a plumber.

Anti-Bullying Strategies

It's common for targets of bullying to feel embarrassed or ashamed. Sometimes they feel like it's their fault—that if they looked or acted differently it wouldn't happen. These feelings are normal and understandable, but they aren't based on the truth and they don't help resolve the situation.

Don't blame yourself

If you're suffering at the hands of a bully, the first thing you should remember is that it's not your fault. You've done nothing wrong. Whatever horrible things the bully may say about you, you have nothing to be ashamed of. You should be proud of who you are. The bully is the one at fault.

Many victims of bullying blame themselves for what is happening.

Walk away, ignore, avoid

Bullies like to feel that they can control their targets' emotions, so it's important not to react angrily or violently. If you fight back, the situation can quickly get out of control. Someone may get hurt, and both you and the bully can end up in trouble. Here are some good strategies for dealing with bullies:

• Say "Stop that!" or "Leave me alone!" in a firm, clear voice.

• Walk away—don't run, even if you're afraid.

• Ignore hurtful remarks—act uninterested; pretend to text someone.

• Avoid the bully—for example, change your route to school or to classes.

• Have a friend with you on the bus, in the hallways, or at recess.

• At the first opportunity, inform a responsible adult, such as a parent, teacher, or school counselor.

Protect yourself

The strategies listed above should help in most situations. However, your safety is always the first priority. If you're under physical attack, it's important to get away and protect yourself. Then, as soon as possible, you should report the incident to a trusted adult.

BULLYING Q & A

Should I fight back?

Q. Every day, on the way to school, I get picked on by this boy at the back of the bus. It began with name-calling, but now he's started poking and kicking me. I told my dad, and he said I should punch the boy in the nose and that'll put an end to it. Trouble is he's way bigger than me, and I'm scared I'll get hurt. What should I do?

A. I don't agree with your dad's advice. As you say, you might get hurt. Even if you win the fight, the bully may then seek revenge later and the situation could get out of control. It's always best to avoid trouble, if you can. Why don't you find a different seat on the bus or make friends with someone else and sit with them? If the bully still makes trouble, tell the driver. Later, once you are at school, tell someone at school, such as a teacher or school counselor, about the problem you had on the bus. You may need to get an adult to intervene in order for the bullying to stop.

The school bus is a common place for bullying to occur.

Practice Self-Control

Bullies like to feel that they have power over other people, so one of the most effective ways of dealing with boys who bully is not to show anger or fear when provoked.

Try to stay calm and confident.

Stay cool

It's very easy to get stressed when faced with a bully. You can prepare for this by practising "cool down" strategies when alone, like counting to 10, taking deep breaths, or keeping a "poker face."

The following tips may help:

• Remember that the bully is an unhappy, frustrated boy who needs help.

• Focus on the positives in your life—the people who love you and your own positive qualities and gifts.

• Find the humor: If you can see the absurdity of the bullying situation and comment on it with humor, you'll become a less interesting target for a bully.

Assert yourself

If ignoring the insults a bully hurls at you doesn't work, try talking to him. Tell him you don't appreciate that kind of talk. Say it firmly and control your emotions. Even saying something nonsensical may work, as it's likely to confuse the bully and leave him wondering why he can't upset you. Try to "own" the insult, and turn it into a positive.

BULLYING Q & A

Who do I turn to?

Q. I've tried walking away and ignoring the bully. I've changed my route around the school to avoid him, but he always seems to find me. Sometimes he takes my money; sometimes he just pushes me around. I've told the teachers, and they punish him, but still he carries on. Any suggestions?

....

A. You need to talk to someone at the school again. Obviously, the punishments have not worked. Ideally, your school would have a school counselor who has been trained in intervention in these situations. Someone who is taking your money is stealing from you, which is a crime. Help your school to see that they need to take this situation more seriously.

Walking away and ignoring bullying can sometimes work.

Find Support

If you are being bullied, ask for help. You could turn to your parents, a teacher, or another trusted adult, such as a minister, priest, or scout master. Sometimes even just talking about a problem can make a difference in how you feel.

Tell an adult

Telling an adult is not being a tattletale. Bullying is wrong and everyone has a duty to speak up about it. If bullies aren't caught and stopped, they'll make other people's lives a misery, too.

Repeat as necessary

Telling an adult will usually end the problem. If it doesn't, and the bullying goes on, you should continue reporting each and every incident. Be as relentless as the bully and tell as many adults as possible until the bullying stops. Work with an adult to keep a record of the bullying—where it happens and what happens—as this evidence may be important in the process of getting it stopped.

Share your problems

Talking with a school counselor or school psychologist is a good idea. Such professionals are trained to help children understand the difference between things they can control (for example, their feelings) and things they cannot (for example, the actions of others).

It might also be helpful to talk about these incidents with friends or other adults. Having trusted people you can turn to for encouragement and support will make the bullying much easier to deal with.

BULLYING Q & A

How do I stop this bullying?

Q. I'm getting bullied by this group of boys at my school. They wait until they see me on my own in the locker room or behind the tennis courts, then they rush out and shove me to the ground. Sometimes they steal my money; other times they kick and punch me. They say they'll kill me if I tell on them. What do I do?

A. Bullies always try to frighten their victims into silence, but don't believe for one minute that staying silent will keep you safe. You have to tell a teacher about this situation. If you're scared, tell the teacher that, too. It's then the school's responsibility to deal with the bullies and to make sure they never hurt or threaten you again.

Bullying and Schools

All schools should have a bullying prevention program.
This could include a school-wide anti-bullying policy,
training for staff and
students, and a bully
hotline, in addition
to support for targets
of bullying.

Anti-bullying policy

The policy should first define
bullying so everyone knows
what it is. It should include
a clear set of guidelines for
staff and students so they
know what to do if they
are targets or witnesses of
bullying, or if a case of bullying is reported to them. It should state how
the school authorities will deal with reports of bullying—how they'll
decide if they're true, how serious they are, and how they'll be punished.

Students in a high
school assembly listen
to an anti-bullying
presentation.

Training

Students and staff are often given training on how to deal with bullying.
This may involve inviting experts in to give assemblies, class talks, and
workshops, or even sending students on a weekend camping retreat. The
aim should be to give practical advice to victims, to encourage bullies
and their followers to change their ways, and to encourage bystanders
to intervene and report bullying.

Reporting bullies

A number should be prominently placed around the school for victims or
witnesses to call or text at any time, with the guarantee that they will
be treated in strict confidence. Or, if your school cannot set up a hotline,
an anonymous "reporting box" could be a way to allow people to report
bullying without fearing the bully will take revenge.

A NEW BROOM

Kevin and his gang liked to lord it over their class. They didn't need to use their fists too often—just once in a while for those who didn't show enough respect. A threat was usually sufficient to get the smaller kids to hand over cash or food. The teachers generally found it easier to turn a blind eye—until the day Mr. Roberts arrived. Mr. Roberts was the new principal and he hated bullying! Kevin and his pals were forced to attend talks encouraging them to change their behavior. Worse, their victims were no longer afraid to tell on them, despite Kevin threatening them with the most unpleasant punishments. Mr. Roberts's arrival was a disaster for Kevin and his bully friends—but great for everyone else!

Stepping In

If you witness someone being bullied, it's important to help him or her in any way you can. You may be able to stop the bullying by saying something to the bully, by gaining other people's support, by going to help the target, or by telling an adult. First, look at the situation carefully, then decide on the best thing to do. Above all, keep yourself safe.

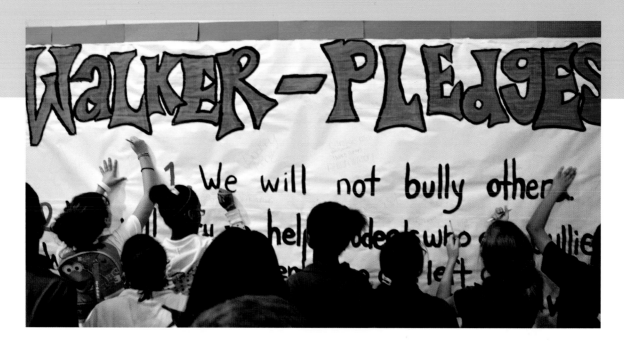

Distract or defuse

You could try to distract the bully to give the target a chance to escape. Or you could try to *defuse the situation* (make the situation less dangerous) with humor, then laugh and encourage others to join in. Alternatively, you could use fear: "Look out, Miss (insert the name of a feared teacher) is on duty." If the bully ignores this or turns on you, you could try and appeal to other bystanders to help you.

Students at a middle school sign a pledge sheet after an assembly kicking off the Olweus anti-bullying program, which focuses on teaching bystanders to take action when they see bullying.

Helping the victim

Always take care before directly intervening in a fight. You could try talking to the person being bullied: "Would you like me to go with you to tell someone about this?" or "Oh, there you are, someone's looking for you." Most importantly, always be kind to someone you know is being bullied. Sitting next to them in the classroom or at lunch signals to the bully that someone is looking out for them.

NOT WALKING ON BY

When Erin saw Susan getting pushed against a locker by a couple of guys, she didn't know what to do. Should she help her or just walk on by and pretend she didn't see anything? Then she saw Susan's face—she looked scared, and there was blood on her cheek. Erin felt angry. She wanted to go and punch the bullies, but knew this wouldn't be a good idea. Forcing herself to be calm, she went over to Susan. "Are you okay?" she asked her. The bullies turned on Erin, calling her "gay" because she was sticking up for another girl. Erin ignored them. "Shall we go and see Mr. Williams?" she asked Susan. Then she took her by the arm and led her to the assistant principal's office. He noted the boys' names. They were both suspended from school.

Joining a target of bullying at lunch helps that person and may gain you a new friend.

How Bullies Can Change

It can be very hard to stop being a bully. There are the rewards that bullying brings: the power, the status, the friends. Don't forget, however, if you are a bully, some of the people you consider friends may not be true friends. They may be friendly towards you because they are afraid of you.

Look at what you're doing

To change, a bully first has to understand what bullying is and accept that he is a bully. If you're a bully, you might excuse your behavior as "teasing" or "having a little fun." To see it for what it is, you have to think about how it must feel to be one of your targets.

Look at yourself

Secondly, you should try to work out why you act in this way. Is it to cover your own weaknesses and insecurities, or because you're unhappy with your life? Perhaps you're being bullied yourself at home? How does it feel when you bully? Do you have a temper problem? Ask yourself, how you would feel if someone did this to you?

Take control

Finally, you must take control of your behavior. When you get the urge to bully someone, you should find a way of stopping yourself—for example, take a deep breath or walk away. You should remove yourself from groups of people who reward you for bullying others, apologize to people you've bullied, and make an effort to treat people with respect. Talking to an adult, such as a school counselor or school psychologist, may allow you to work through some of your own feelings.

It can be hard to come to terms with the fact that you are a bully.

A LIFE-CHANGING BOOK

Gavin was in trouble again. He'd been sent to the isolation room at his school after bullying a couple of girls. Angry and bored, he picked up a book that was lying on the table. The cover showed a huge white bear towering over a boy armed with a knife. The book, called *Touching Spirit Bear* by Ben Mikaelsen, was about a violent boy sent to a remote Alaskan island as a punishment. Gavin began to read about the boy's quest to kill a white bear he'd seen on the island. The boy ended up suffering terrible injuries, and his attempt to turn himself into a better person had a powerful effect on Gavin. The book showed him that he was a bully and that he had anger-management problems, just like the boy in the story. With help from his teachers and parents, Gavin started to change. He apologized to his victims, and he now does his best to help those weaker than himself.

Building Confidence

Bullying is partly a power game in which boys tend to pick on people who they perceive as "weaker" than themselves. It's true that targets of bullying often have low self-esteem or lack self-confidence. Building confidence is one strategy that can be used to counter bullying.

Body language

When you walk around, look up. Looking at your feet sends a message to bullies that you're fearful—and this can make you a target. Smiling and looking people in the eye when you talk to them projects confidence. And it's amazing how acting confidently can help you actually *feel* confident.

Make new friends

Bullies tend to pick on people with few friends. If you're a target of bullying, it helps to have a group of trusted friends for support. Join a club or society so you can meet people who share your interests. Try not to be shy about going up and talking to people for the first time. Most people are naturally friendly. If they're not, it means you didn't need them anyway.

Don't forget

Once you've gained some self-confidence, hopefully your days of being bullied will be behind you. But don't forget to keep an eye out for others who may still be suffering. You know what they're going through and maybe you can offer them the friendship they so badly need.

BULLYING Q & A

Quit calling me stupid...

Q. Whenever I see Jake coming towards me, I know what's going to happen. He's going to say I'm stupid. Just because I've got a learning disability, he's always trying to get people to laugh at me—and most times they do. I know I'll never be cool. I'll never be able to think of clever things to say back to him. The only time I'm happy is when I'm on my own, playing my guitar. What can I do?

....

A. My advice is: keep practising your guitar. Becoming talented at something boosts confidence. Why not try joining a band so you can meet some like-minded people? All those guys who laugh at you right now—if they heard you play, maybe you'd win their respect, and their friendship. Then the laugh will be on Jake for calling you "stupid."

Young boys in Florida attend a class to learn to deal with potential bullying. The class is focused on self-defense and exercises designed to build self-confidence.

Additional Resources

Websites

http://www.anti-bullyingalliance.org/
A United Kingdom-based alliance of organizations that works to stop bullying and create safer environments.

http://www.bullying.org
A Canadian organization that provides educational programs and resources to individuals, families, educational institutions, and organizations.

http://www.bullypolice.org
A U.S. watchdog organization advocating for bullied children and reporting on state anti-bullying laws.

http://www.cdc.gov/bam/life/index.html
A Centers for Disease Control and Prevention (CDC) site for young adults about dealing with bullying, peer pressure, and stress.

http://www.thecoolspot.gov/pressures.asp
A site created by the U.S. National Institute on Alcohol Abuse and Alcoholism (NIAAA) for kids 11-13 years old.

https://www.facebook.com/safety/bullying
A campaign by Facebook and other sponsors asking everyone to show their support and spread the word against bullying. This page also has advice for people receiving abusive posts on Facebook.

http://www.itgetsbetter.org/
What began as a single YouTube video by author Dan Savage that encouraged young LGBT youth to tough it out through school, is now a website featuring thousands of videos made by youths and by celebrities attesting that life gets easier for LGBT people in adulthood.

http://www.ncpc.org/topics/bullying
A National Crime Prevention Council website, includes a page about girls and bullying.

http://www.nobully.com
An organization that helps schools to implement an anti-bullying program.

http://www.pacer.org/bullying/
PACER's National Bullying Prevention Center unites, engages, and educates communities nationwide to address bullying through creative, relevant, and interactive resources. PACER's bullying prevention resources are designed to benefit all students, including students with disabilities.

http://pbskids.org/itsmylife/
PBS advice site about issues that include family, friends, school, and emotions.

http://solutionsforbullying.com/Associations.html
Resources for parents, teachers, and other professionals listing organizations in different countries as a starting point for getting help.

http://www.stopbullying.gov/
A U.S. Department of Health & Human Services website with lots of information for kids, teens, parents, and educators.

http://www.violencepreventionworks.org/
A site for the Olweus Bullying Prevention Program, an American program that has been proven to reduce bullying in schools.

Books

How to Beat Physical Bullying (Beating Bullying series) by Alexandra Handon-Harding (Rosen Central, 2013)

Bullies, Cyberbullies and Frenemies (Teen Life Confidential series) by Michelle Elliott (Wayland, 2013)

Bullying (Teen Issues series) by Lori Hile (Heinemann 2012)

Bullying Under Attack: True Stories Written by Teen Victims, Bullies & Bystanders by Stephanie Meyer, John Meyer, Emily Sperber and Heather Alexander (Health Communications, Inc., 2013)

The Bullying Workbook for Teens: Activities to Help You Deal with Social Aggression and Cyberbullying by Raychelle Cassada Lohmann and Julia V. Taylor (New Harbinger Publications, 2013)

Confessions of a Former Bully by Trudy Ludwig (Tricycle Press, 2010)

The Courage to Be Yourself: True Stories by Teens About Cliques, Conflicts, and Overcoming Peer Pressure edited by Al Desetta and Educators for Social Responsibility (Free Spirit Publishing, 2005)

The Drama Years: Real Girls Talk About Surviving Middle School – Bullies, Brands, Body Image, and More by Haley Kilpatrick and Whitney Joiner (Free Press, 2012)

Friendship Troubles (A Smart Girl's Guide series) by Patti Kelley Criswell (American Girl Publishing, revised edition, 2013)

A Guys' Guide to Conflict/A Girls' Guide to Conflict (Flip-It-Over Guides to Teen Emotions) by Jim Gallagher and Dorothy Kavanaugh (Enslow Publishers, 2008)

Hot Issues, Cool Choices: Facing Bullies, Peer Pressure, Popularity, and Put-downs by Sandra Mcleod Humphrey (Prometheus Books, 2007)

lol...OMG!: What Every Student Needs to Know About Online Reputation Management, Digital Citizenship, and Cyberbullying by Matt Ivester (Serra Knight Publishing, 2011)

Online Bullying (Teen Mental Health series) by Peter Ryan (Rosen 2012)

Peer Pressure (Issues that Concern You series) edited by Lorraine Savage (Greenhaven Press, 2009)

Peer Pressure (Tough Topics series) by Elizabeth Raum (Heinemann Library, 2008)

Physical Bullying (Take a Stand Against Bullying series) by Jennifer Rivkin (Crabtree Publishing, 2013)

Queen Bees and Wannabes by Rosalind Wiseman (Piatkus 2002; rev. edition, Three Rivers Press, 2009)

Teen Cyberbullying Investigated: Where Do Your Rights End and Consequences Begin? by Thomas A. Jacobs (Free Spirit Publishing, 2010)

Helplines (USA)

Boys Town National Hotline: 1-800-448-3000 (available to all children; toll- free)

Child-Help USA: 1-800-422-4453 (24-hour toll-free)

National Suicide Prevention Lifeline: 1-800-273-TALK (1-888-628-9454, for Spanish-speaking callers; 24-hour toll-free)

Glossary

anti-bullying policies an agreed upon set of rules or actions to stop bullying

birth order a person's age in relation to the ages of his or her siblings (for example, being the youngest or oldest child in a family); psychologists believe birth order has an effect on personality

bystander someone who watches an event but who does not intervene

cyberbullying using such information technologies as e-mail, cell phones, and instant messaging to send harmful messages

desensitized having become accustomed to hurtful behavior

direct aggression openly aggressive behavior, such as kicking, hitting, or name-calling

eating disorder an illness related to ideas and behaviors about food and body image

exclusion being deliberately left out

gay homosexual; feeling sexually attracted to a person of the same sex (gay is a term more commonly used for men than women)

gender group a set of people of the same sex

hazing initiation ceremonies that can often be dangerous and abusive in nature

homophobia a fear of, or prejudice against, people who are homosexuals

indirect aggression a kind of quiet and sneaky aggressive behavior; it could involve such actions as spreading rumors or blaming a target for something he or she did not do

isolation feeling apart from or unlike other people

lesbian a woman who is sexually attracted to women

LGBT initials that stand for lesbian, gay, bisexual, and transgender

peer pressure feeling that you should do, think, or say something because that's what others your age are doing

relational aggression a type of bullying in which the bully tries to harm the target by damaging the target's friendships or lowering the target's social status

sibling rivalry fighting, disagreements, and competition between siblings (brothers and/ or sisters)

social status how popular a person is, usually defined by the people around them

transgender a person who does not identify with the gender assigned to them at birth; for example, someone born as a male child may grow up feeling female and wear clothing and take on behaviors associated with female children

Index

Acknowledgments

Cover photo: Alamy Images (Damien VC)
Back cover photo: Shutterstock (kaarsten)

Alamy 13 (Steve Skjold), 33 (PhotoAlto sas), 38 (ZUMA Press, Inc).

Corbis 8-9 bottom (Radius Images), 10, 11 (Adrian Wilson), 12-13 (William Gottlieb), 23 (Creasource), 24 (Don Hammond/Design Pics), 25 and 31 (Will & Deni McIntyre), 27 Laurence Mouton/PhotoAlto), 28 (Anderson Ross/Blend Images), 34 (BURGER/ phanie/Phanie Sarl), 35 (Weston Colton/Rubberball), 37 (Mike Kemp/Rubberball), 39, 43 (Damon Higgins/ ZUMA Press).

Shutterstock 4-5 (Mandy Godbehear), 6 and 16 (ejwhite), 7 (Piotr Zajac), 8-9 top (dotshock), 14 (Andrey Shadrin), 15 and 40 (Blend Images), 17 (RimDream), 18-19 and 41 (Monkey Business Images), 20 (Lisa F. Young), 21 (Junial Enterprises), 22 (muzsy), 26 (Melissa Hanes), 29 (Themalni), 30 (Maya Kruchankova), 32 (V.S. Anandhakrishna), 36 (Michael Chamberlin), 42 (Solovyova Lyudmyla).